Folk Tale Plays
From Around the World
—That Kids Will Love!

By Marci Appelbaum and Jeff Catanese

S C H O L A S T I C
PROFESSIONAL BOOKS

New York • Toronto • London • Auckland • Sydney
Mexico City • New Delhi • Hong Kong • Buenos Aires

Dedications

Jeff would like to dedicate this book to his co-author Marci, who is his co-author in so many ways.

To Jeff, with love and appreciation for all that you have taught me.   —M.A.

Acknowledgments

We would like to thank Sarah Longhi for her help, support and friendship, Attic Salt Theatre Company, whose talented actors helped shape the plays in this book, and Jennifer Barnhart for inadvertantly making this book possible.

Cover design by SOLÁS Design & Production

Interior design by Sydney Wright

Cover art and interior illustrations by Margeaux Lucas

Map design on page 71 by Jim McMahon

ISBN: 0-439-22257-5

Contents

Introduction

"Once upon a time . . ." is a phrase that every child learns at a very young age. Story-telling—including the retelling of traditional folk tales—lays important foundations for children's learning. Folk tales feature predictable narrative patterns and characters with emphasized traits, which help youngsters understand story structure and easily distinguish between fantastic and realistic elements. These cultural tales also teach "global" lessons in behavior and etiquette with humor instead of didacticism and offer older students a way to reject stereotypes and explore their own or other cultures.

Despite the old-fashioned characters, dialogue, and settings that we may find in tradi-tional folk tales, there is, in fact, a place for these stories in our fast-paced, modern world. Witness the number of feature-length movies based on traditional folk tales, or the new urban legends and myths that regularly fill our e-mail in-boxes and you'll see that folk tales continue to be a powerful force in our culture and communication.

We consider a *folk tale* to be any story that a people or culture has adopted. These stories include the morality tales, fool's tales, trickster tales, fairy tales, and other forms that you'll find in this book. But folk tales may also include any jokes, riddles, anecdotes, ghost stories, or other story form that is commonly passed down through word of mouth. The people or culture that shares these folk tales can be as large as a continent or as small as a family—we often learn our favorite folk tales from the people closest to us.

So, why did we choose to write a book of folk tale plays? When we formed Attic Salt Theatre Company in 1998, we sought ways to bring theater to children. We drew on our backgrounds in playwriting, directing, acting, and education to create original plays that engaged kids in the arts and encouraged the exploration of diverse cultures. We wanted to design a theater experience that was not only appropriate for children, but that also had a small production budget and would enhance multicultural and cross-curricular programs at schools. Finally, we wanted to present interesting stories that would make our audiences laugh and be amazed. The obvious source material was the stories that met those criteria when we were children—folk tales.

The secret to writing this book was to make it fun and interesting for us. We selected those elements that belonged to each story's original form and purpose, and then we added humor with jokes and rhymes and scary asides. We have included some staging suggestions for each play, too, but we encourage you to allow students to think of ways to solve simple staging problems.

We hope that you and your students will read these folk tale plays in the same spirit of fun and curiosity in which they were written!

—*Jeff and Marci*

How to Use This Book

Each chapter includes background information on the featured story and country of origin, followed by the play and related activities that encourage students to further explore the ideas and themes presented. The activities target key objectives in reading, writing, social studies, math, science, and, of course, theater. Additionally, we have listed resources on each activity page that can be used to enhance the suggested activities or any other lesson plans that you may create.

Reading Levels

These plays are designed to accommodate a variety of reading levels. Every play includes a suggested vocabulary review with helpful definitions and pronunciation guides for those words that may be unfamiliar. The plays also offer a variety of roles that provide appropriate reading challenges for readers at different levels. The part of the Storyteller (the narrator), for example, poses a greater challenge than that of a secondary character, who speaks less or has a nonspeaking role. Given these different reading levels, students may participate at a level that best suits their ability. Note that two of the plays, "Tangled-up Feet" and "The Monkey and the Crocodile," are written at a slightly lower reading level overall than some of the others, and may be better suited for less-fluent readers.

Fully Staged Version or Group Read-Aloud

Being "theater people" ourselves, we're convinced of the value of using plays to explore theater with your students. Thus, each chapter includes staging ideas for the featured play. Our staging tips and theater activities offer ways to help students create simple, but thoughtful, props and costumes and solve other theater-related problems creatively, such as how to show a water setting in "The Monkey and the Crocodile"—without using water. In fact, staging of any of these plays could be made very simple with a little imagination. Let students think of ways to solve simple staging problems. (Remember, in the schoolyard they create battlefields and palaces, and make themselves the soldiers and princesses that inhabit them!)

Alternatives to fully staging each play include reading a play aloud as a whole class with groups of two or three students reading a single part chorally, or assigning the play (or different plays!) to small groups, so that every student can assume the role of a character. Allow laughter, invite questions, and encourage students to find a unique way of presenting and reading the plays. We have designed follow-up activities that build on this kind of experimental atmosphere, and we encourage you to adapt the activities in a way that helps trigger your students' curiosity—and will have them asking to read the next play right away.

The Sultan's Wife

BACKGROUND

This tale—the story of a lonely sultan who tries to buy his wife happiness—was originally told in Eastern Africa. Over time, nomadic groups passing through the region helped to spread this folk tale throughout the vast Sahara desert. (A new story must have seemed as good as gold to a weary traveler!) Notice the influence of the nomadic life on the story: even the high-ranking sultan lives in a tent.

STAGING TIPS

In the staging of this tale, you may wish to allow students to find materials and props that help represent their ideas of what the sultan's tent or his "golden robes" might look like. But keep in mind that even without props, students can mime some of these elaborate costume and setting ideas, such as lifting a heavy curtain when entering the sultan's tent or draping several layers of royal robes over one's shoulders. How these things look is then limited only by the imaginations of the actors and audience.

VOCABULARY

sultan: A king or sovereign, especially in a Muslim country.

nomad: A person with no fixed home who travels from place to place.

traditions: Any customs that are passed down through family or cultural connections.

oral tradition: Any story, joke, or other tale that is told from memory and passed down through family or cultural connections.

generation

tongue

casserole

The Sultan's Wife

◆ CHARACTERS ◆

The Storyteller
Sultan
Sultan's Wife
Servant

Poor Man
Poor Man's Wife
Butcher

The Storyteller: The folk tales we know from hundreds of years ago were not actually written. Well, eventually someone wrote them down, but most of them started as *oral traditions*. That is, stories were told from memory and handed down from generation to generation. This one came from Eastern Africa, and was told in Swahili, a language that was spoken in many parts of Africa at one time. The people who first told this story were nomads, and they probably told tales like this to pass the time as they traveled across vast deserts.

A long time ago, in the middle of the desert, there lived a powerful sultan. He had everything that money could possibly buy. He had a

great tent and servants and cooks and jewels and more food and riches than you could imagine. It seemed that he should be quite happy, but instead, the sultan spent most of his time feeling miserable.

Servant: Master, I have chosen your wardrobe for today. I heard that you woke up feeling miserable again this morning. I thought perhaps you would feel better if you were wearing your golden robes.

Sultan: Oh, yes, yes, my golden robes. Yes, I suppose that will be fine.

Servant: Did you sleep well last night on your 100 comfy pillows?

Sultan: Sleep? Yes, yes, but when I woke this morning, I found myself to be alone. And at breakfast this morning, I had a feast fit for a sultan, but I had no one to share it with. I don't know what is wrong with me—perhaps I have the flu. I feel hot. It's very warm in here.

Servant: That is because this is the desert, sire. It is always warm in here. It sounds like you are lonely.

Sultan: Lonely? How absurd! I am not lonely. I just wish I had someone else around here to keep me company.

The Storyteller: And so the sultan decided to marry. He wed the most beautiful and healthy woman in the kingdom. He wanted to keep her happy and healthy, so he gave her everything that money could buy. But as the months passed, the sultan's wife had begun to grow unhappy. The sultan gave her everything, but he didn't talk to her much.

Sultan: Have you noticed how often she just sits there and looks sad?

Servant: Yup. She just sits there and looks sad. That's almost all she does anymore.

Sultan: She used to look so healthy. She smiled and she looked strong. But now she has withered away to practically nothing. Maybe she has the flu. Dear, do you feel warm?

Sultan's Wife: (*Sadly.*) This is the desert. I always feel warm here.

Sultan: Perhaps it's because she eats hardly anything. You cannot look

healthy when you have almost nothing to eat.

Servant: I don't think that's true, sire. You know that little poor man in the tent next door? Well, he and his wife live off nothing but crumbs, and she's the happiest woman I've ever seen!

Sultan: Really? Well, perhaps I just haven't been giving my wife enough jewels to wear. You cannot be happy if you don't have the proper amount of jewels to wear.

Servant: Nope, I really don't think that's it either. The man from next door— his wife doesn't have any jewels at all. She has nothing to wear except rags, but does she ever look happy!

Sultan: Well, it seems that man from next door knows something that I do not. Perhaps I should pay him a visit and see this wonderful wife of his.

The Storyteller: And with that, the sultan traveled next door to see the poor man and his wife.

Poor Man: Hello, sire. It is a great honor to have you here.

Sultan: I come here in need of your help.

Poor Man: Our help? I can't imagine how . . .

Sultan: It's about your wife.

Poor Man's Wife: About me?

Sultan: Oh, yes! I have heard that you are one of the happiest people around here!

Poor Man's Wife: You have? Well, I am pretty happy.

Sultan: I also have a wife, but lately she has not been very happy. Your wife is obviously happy and healthy. Since you don't have money and jewels and fancy foods to give her, you must have some secret to keeping her happy. What is it?

Poor Man: Well, I guess I just make sure that she gets whatever food we can afford . . . and we drink lots of water. Um . . . We walk in the sun a lot.

That seems to give her pleasure. And um . . . What else? Oh, yes! I almost forgot the most important thing! (*Points to his own tongue.*) "Meat of the tongue."

(*The Sultan looks confused.*)

Sultan: Of course! How could I forget that part? (*Points to his own tongue.*) Silly me! The most important part! Yes, yes, thank you. You have been most helpful!

The Storyteller: And so the sultan, thinking he knew the secret, called on the butcher.

Butcher: You wanted to see me, sire?

Sultan: Yes. I need the tongues of all of the slaughtered animals from your butcher shop.

Butcher: *All* of them, sire? Most people prefer cow tongues, but not . . . Whatever you say, sire.

The Storyteller: For the next full year, the sultan's wife ate tongue every night. Steamed tongue, fried tongue, roast tongue, any kind of tongue you could imagine. But she never got any happier.

Sultan: I don't understand it. I did everything the man from next door told me to do. My wife drinks lots of water and enjoys the morning walks that she takes by herself. I make sure that she gets at least one healthy serving of tongue a day. But still, she is sad and sick and she cries a lot.

Servant: Maybe you should talk to the peasant man again. He might have another suggestion.

Sultan: Maybe I should do more than just talk to him. Maybe I should let my

wife stay with him for a while. Then he could fix her all up. Maybe he knows some magic or something. Maybe a spell to spin on her . . . or a potion he puts in the tongue . . .

Servant: Potion, sire?

Sultan: Well, it's got to be something . . .

The Storyteller: And thinking that he had found the best possible solution, the sultan took his wife to the poor man.

Sultan: I need your help again. Your wife—she's still happy?

Poor Man's Wife: Happy as I've ever been, sire.

Sultan: I did everything you said, but my wife is still miserable. So, I have decided—my wife should come and stay with you!

Poor Man: With me?

Sultan: Yes, just until she's feeling better.

Poor Man's Wife: That would be wonderful!

Poor Man: Sire, I don't mean to be disrespectful. I would be honored to help you and your wife, but where will she sleep? There's hardly enough room in this tent for two of us. And there's certainly not enough food for an extra person.

Poor Man's Wife: I know! Perhaps I could stay with you, sire, just until your wife feels better.

The Storyteller: So the sultan's wife stayed with the poor man, and the poor man's wife went off to live in the sultan's tent. Time went by, and the sultan's wife had grown strong and healthy again, but now the poor man's happy wife had become sickly and sad.

Sultan: I don't understand this at all. I've done everything that I was supposed to do. You have a nice room with comfy pillows and you have walks in the sunshine. You have all of the jewels you could possibly want. What is the problem?

Poor Man's Wife: When I lived with my husband, we didn't have much food. We slept on the hard floor. We certainly didn't have any jewels. But it didn't matter because he gave me the "meat of the tongue." *That's* why I was always so happy.

Sultan: But I have given you the meat of every tongue in this kingdom!

Poor Man's Wife: I don't want to *eat* tongue. My husband talks to me. He tells wonderful stories. We laugh together until we fall off our stools . . . And we sing. You've been busy feeding me tongue casserole, but you have hardly said more than 20 words to me since I arrived here. Of course I'm sad. I'm lonely.

Sultan: I did the same thing to my wife.

Poor Man's Wife: You can fix things. You just have to talk to your wife and spend time with her.

Sultan: I can do that! I have to get her back right away!

The Storyteller: The sultan ran over to the poor man's tent to tell his wife what he had learned.

Sultan: Hello! Hello! Please let us in!

Poor Man: Welcome, sire. How can I help you?

Sultan: (*to his wife*) My darling, I have made a terrible mistake. Meat of the tongue! Meat of the tongue! I have never *talked* to you! That's what I have been doing wrong all of this time!

Sultan's Wife: Meat of the tongue. I knew you'd figure it out.

The Storyteller: The sultan's wife was overjoyed and gladly went back to her own home, where she and the sultan talked and laughed and sang together, and she stayed happy and healthy for the rest of her life. Oh, and tongue was *never* served in the kingdom again.

The Sultan's Wife

SOCIAL STUDIES ◆ *Family Stories*

In the same way that countries and regions pass along stories through oral tradition, every family has an oral tradition of its own. Ask each student to tell a short story about something that happened in his or her family long ago and has been passed down. Discuss what has happened to the students in their lives that they might pass down to their children and grandchildren. What lessons did the old stories teach? What lessons might the students' stories teach? Think of times that families might take the opportunity to tell these stories.

LANGUAGE ARTS
◆ *How Languages Form*

Stories gather and spread new words and ideas as they pass from culture to culture. And languages grow as stories are shared. What foreign words has the English language adopted? Encourage students to think of the words they know. Can students identify the languages from which the words come? Show students how to use the entry information from a college dictionary to find a word's origin. If students are aware of their ethnic backgrounds, encourage them to identify words that their family's culture has introduced to English. How about new words they would like to introduce to the language of the classroom? On a large world outline map, you and your students can write the new words from the discussion in the country of origin.

Keep the map up in the classroom and add new words as you come across them.

THEATER ◆ *Invisible Gifts*

Give each student a lump of invisible clay. Ask them to play with the clay and shape it into an object that their favorite character might need (for example, the sultan might need a new turban, the servant might need a new broom, etc.). Discuss each student's gift. How can you show what the gift is by how heavy it is? How can you show what shape it is? How can you show what material it is made of?

HEALTH ◆ *Foods From Home*

Chances are that your students have never tasted tongue like the sultan feeds his wife in this play. Some may even think it's strange or gross! However, tongue is considered a delicacy in many cultures. Host a special foods day in the classroom, to which students may bring or describe a new food that they've tried or read about but that they don't usually eat. Sharing food is an excellent way to help students explore and appreciate different cultures as well as their own.

◆ RESOURCES ◆

You can find many African recipes on the Web. Here is one fun page: www.lifeinafrica.com/fun/recipes/.

Jambo Means Hello: Swahili Alphabet Book by Muriel L. Feelings (Puffin Pied Piper, 1981).

The Golden Reed Pipe

BACKGROUND

"The Golden Reed Pipe" is a Chinese hero tale that is partially told in verse. Many cultures transmit folk tales in verse, as rhymes make it easier to remember the order of events and details of the story. Verse tales are often found in Chinese folklore, which leads us to believe that verse was at one time a popular oral tradition style in the East, just as it was popular in Europe during the 1500s and in Greece around 400 B.C. In order to illustrate this common storytelling device, several of the characters in this play speak in verse.

Like the Grimm's tale of "Little Red Riding Hood," this story features a character named Little Red. She is known by this name because she wears red. As folklore has passed from culture to culture we find such similarities in many stories. As a matter of fact, Little Red stories became popular throughout the world in the eighteenth, nineteenth, and twentieth centuries.

VOCABULARY	
myth	guardians
gale	bayberry
boulder	obstacle
troublesome	summit
ferocious	cinder
chiseling	torment
writhing	exhausted
laurels	

STAGING TIPS

Remind students that all of the props in this play can be mimed. The rakes used by the mother and Little Red, the boulder, and even the reed pipe can be mimed. You might also try using a paper towel tube as the pipe and have someone offstage make the music with a slide whistle or by singing. To depict his huge size, challenge a small group of students to build (or simply move as) the dragon (the tail, the body, the arms and legs, and the head). Have the students work together to create and orchestrate how the dragon moves.

Chinese Dragon

MATERIALS

Cardboard (precut, clean circular pizza-box inserts work well!)
Construction paper, glitter, markers, or other decorative materials
Rulers (one for each student who will be operating the dragon)
Heavy-duty tape
Hole puncher
Thick yarn or string (any color)
Large bed sheet

WHAT TO DO

1. Cut cardboard into 18"- to 24"-diameter circles. Make one circle for each student who will operate the dragon. One circle should be larger than the others; this will serve as the front or face piece.

2. Encourage students to decorate the face piece and each circle creatively (have them consider what sections of the dragon's body their circles will be). The dragon can be as scary, funny, or decorative as they like.

3. Tape a ruler or 1-foot-long stick to the back of each circle. Half of it should be attached to the circle so that the remaining six inches can be used as a handle. Students can now line up and move their circles independently to give their dragon movement.

Follow the steps below if you and your students want the movement of the dragon to be more coordinated. (A long piece of string or yarn keeps the dragon together while still allowing each part some independent movement.)

4. On the right side of each circle, about two inches from the edge, punch two holes. These holes should be one on top of the other (vertical), about two inches apart.

5. Repeat step 3 on the left side of each circle. Now every circle should have four holes in it, two on the left side and two on the right.

6. Thread one very long piece of string or yarn through the bottom right hole on each circle, beginning with the face piece. When all of the circles have been strung together, thread the same piece of string back through the top right side holes of every circle and knot both ends at the face piece. (Each part of the dragon should be about two feet apart, so be sure to adjust the length of your yarn proportionately—e.g., if there are going to be five parts of the dragon, the whole dragon will be eight feet long, so you will need a 16-foot piece of yarn for each side.)

7. Using a second piece of string, thread the holes and knot the yarn on the left side in the same way.

8. Have students practice moving their dragon around the room. It's like a game of follow the leader. Encourage them to try different positions. Ask how they might move when the dragon is talking, walking, or dancing.

The Golden Reed Pipe

◆ CHARACTERS ◆

The Storyteller   Mother
Little Red   Bayberry
Crow   Dragon
Lizards, Worms, and Frogs

The Storyteller: Many tales tell of magical beasts and how to overcome them. In China that beast in most stories was the dragon. Dragons looked a little like lizards, but they could fly and they breathed fire. The myth of dragons spread to Europe, where dragons were known as keepers or guardians of treasure. A scary story in ancient China might be about the trouble that a dragon caused a town, and a hero story might be about how a dragon was beaten. This is one of those stories. It begins with Little Red, a girl who always wears red clothes, and her mother while they are hard at work plowing a field.

(*Mother and Little Red rake and plow a field.*)

Little Red: Working in the field is so much easier with my wonderful brother to help us.

Mother: Little Red, sometimes I think that you've been working too hard. You have no brother.

Little Red: Oh, but Mother, I do.

The Storyteller: At that moment a gale blew up around them, and they saw in the sky an evil dragon. Though they ran as hard as they could, the dragon caught up to Little Red and lifted her into the sky.

Little Red: (*Yelling.*) Oh Mother, oh Mother, as dear as can be! My brother, my brother will come rescue me!

The Storyteller: The mother could barely hear Little Red as the dragon carried her off. She sadly headed home to figure out what to do.

Mother: Oh, my goodness. What can I do to save my baby, Little Red? If only she really did have a brother, he could help.

(*Mother starts to struggle against the shrubbery in her path.*)

Mother: I don't remember all these bushes being here before. The laurels and bayberries are getting caught in my hair and stuck on my dress.

The Storyteller: The mother was able to get free of the bayberry bushes, but when she got home she discovered someone was already there. A boy of about fourteen years stood in the middle of the room.

Mother: Who are you?

Bayberry: Hello, Mother, I'm your son.

Mother: But I have no son.

Bayberry: You do now.

The Storyteller: The mother took a good look and noticed that the boy had very red skin and a very round face.

Mother: You must have come from that bayberry bush.

Bayberry: I think that I did, Mother.

Mother: Then you are my son, and I will call you Bayberry.

The Storyteller: The mother thought about asking Bayberry to rescue his sister, but she wouldn't dare to ask such a sweet, young child to take on such a dangerous task. Then a few days later a crow flew into the window of the house.

Crow: Your sister suffers much out there! She's weeping in the dragon's lair!

Bayberry: What do you mean, *my sister?*

Crow: The dragon has your Little Red! He'll make her dig until she's dead!

(The crow flies away. Bayberry runs to his mother.)

Bayberry: Mother, do I have a sister?

Mother: Yes, my boy, you do. She was called Little Red, because she loved to dress in red. An evil dragon came and took her away.

(Bayberry picks up a big stick.)

Bayberry: I'm going to rescue Little Red and destroy that evil dragon. Then he can't do any more harm!

The Storyteller: As sad as the mother was to see her son go, she helped him prepare for the journey and saw him off. He walked for many days, over the plains and up into the mountains. One day he came upon a giant boulder that blocked his path.

Bayberry: This is my first obstacle! If I don't remove it now, it will cause trouble for many more people after me.

(Bayberry thrusts his stick under the boulder and heaves with all his might, and with a great "crack" his stick breaks in two. Then he tries to move it with his hands, and, using all his strength, rolls the boulder down the valley.)

Bayberry: That boulder was more troublesome than I imagined. Now I must . . . Wait a minute. What's this? A beautiful golden reed pipe.

(Bayberry picks up the pipe that was under the rock and gives it a try. It makes a beautiful sound and instantly plays a light melody. Suddenly all of the worms, frogs, and lizards nearby begin to wiggle and dance. There is movement all around Bayberry. He stops playing and the movement stops. He plays again and the movement is wilder than ever. He stops.)

Bayberry: This reed pipe must be magic. When I play it, all the earthworms, frogs, and lizards by the roadside begin to dance. The quicker the tune I play, the faster the creatures dance. When I stop, they stop. Ah! Now I have an idea about how to deal with that evil dragon!

The Storyteller: Bayberry continued to the very summit of the mountain, where he saw a ferocious-looking dragon curled up at the entrance to a cave. Bones were all around the cave, and every bush and tree nearby was burnt to a cinder. But he also saw his beautiful sister, her red clothing torn, chiseling away at the cave entrance.

Little Red: Please, Mister Dragon, please let me go! I've worked so hard, and I miss my mother so!

Dragon: You're ungrateful, Mistress Red! I told you: to me you'll be wed! Now finish carving out my house! Until then: QUIET, as a mouse!

Bayberry: Wicked monster! Get away! You won't torment her one more day!

Dragon: To torment, sir, I don't intend! Come closer now and be my friend!

Bayberry: Your friendship I will never know, for on this pipe I'll blow and blow.

(Bayberry begins to blow on his golden reed pipe. The music sets the evil dragon dancing despite himself. Little Red puts down her chisel and runs from the cave. Bayberry blows a quicker tune, and the evil dragon continues to dance, squirming and writhing even faster.)

Little Red: Oh, my brother. I knew you would come and rescue me. Thank you! Thank you!

(Bayberry continues to blow on the pipe and the dragon continues dancing.)

Little Red: Brother, it's me, Little Red. Why won't you talk to me?

(Bayberry points frantically to the pipe, indicating that he can't stop playing. The dragon is exhausted, with steam coming out of his nostrils.)

Dragon: Away, away! You are the stronger! Blow no more! Torture me no longer! I concede now you have won! You and your pipe, leave me alone!

The Storyteller: But Bayberry had no intention of stopping. He kept that dragon dancing and led him right into the middle of a big lake nearby.

Dragon: Leave me alone, and I'll stay in this lake! I don't want to die, make no mistake!

Bayberry: You now know my power, so don't have a doubt, I'll be back to finish you if you ever come out.

(The dragon nods his head and sinks into the lake.)

The Storyteller: Bayberry and Little Red hugged each other out of the joy of being reunited, even though they had just met for the first time, and they happily headed for home.

(There is the sound of intense splashing, and the dragon flies out of the lake with its fangs and claws ready to strike.)

Little Red: Brother, you gave him a chance, but please don't give it twice! It was a mistake to think he'd be nice!

(Bayberry blows on the reed pipe once again.)

Dragon: Oh, no. Here we go again.

(The dragon dances frantically, and falls back into the water.)

The Storyteller: It may sound hard to believe, but Bayberry stood on the shore of that lake, and blew that reed pipe for seven days straight. He blew until the dragon tired out and couldn't dance any longer. Then the dragon couldn't even stand. And finally the dragon just sank right into the lake; its evil days had come to an end.

Little Red: Let's go home now.

Bayberry: Mother will be thrilled to see that you're all right.

The Storyteller: The children traveled home as quickly as they could, and their mother was very happy to see them. And word of Bayberry and his magical reed pipe must have gotten around, because no dragon ever appeared in that part of China again.

The Golden Reed Pipe

SOCIAL STUDIES ◆ *Chinese Zodiac*

In this story, the dragon is evil and causes trouble; however, the dragon is usually a symbol of authority, luck, and wisdom in China. Have students use a book or Web site (see Resources) to find out which symbol of the Chinese zodiac they were born under.

LANGUAGE ARTS ◆ *Magic Objects*

Many folk tales endow ordinary objects with magical properties. Have the class brainstorm a list of everyday objects that could be substituted for the reed pipe, and thus change the course of events in the story. For example, if Bayberry finds a thumbtack, it might have magical powers to stick on command. How could Bayberry use it to defeat the dragon? Each student should pick an object from the list, decide what magical power it will have, and write a paragraph that begins where Bayberry finds this object (in place of the reed pipe). You might provide the following starter: *When Bayberry had pushed the giant boulder aside, he found a magical _____. When he _____ it, he discovered it could . . .* Be sure to share and compare imaginative objects and solutions to this tale!

THEATER ◆ *Designing Costumes*

Discuss how you might use different costumes to depict the characters in the play. How could you dress Bayberry to look more like a berry? What would the dragon's costume look like? How could you easily make these costumes from clothes that you already have? What might Little Red be wearing to work in the field? What could you add to make it look like a traditional Chinese outfit?

POETRY ◆ *Translating Texts*

In this folk tale play, some of the characters speak in verse. Tie this story in to a lesson on poetry. Discuss types of poetry and rhyme schemes. Ask the students to each take a few sentences from a well-known story, like "The Three Little Pigs," and rewrite them in verse. For younger students, try this writing activity as a group and provide the first line of the couplet: *Once upon a time lived the three little pigs . . .* (possible response: *One made a house of straw, another of twigs*). Record the verses on chart paper. Do the rhymes make the stories more interesting? More confusing?

◆ RESOURCES ◆

China by Diana Granat and Stanlee Brimberg (Scholastic Professional Books, 1999) Background information, hands-on activities, maps, and reproducibles. Grades 4 and up.

Chinese Zodiac at http://central.k12.ca.us/akers/zodiac.html offers up simple definitions of each "personality type" of the Chinese zodiac.

The Dragon's Tale and Other Animal Fables of the Chinese Zodiac by Demi (Henry Holt, 1996).

Good Luck Gold and Other Poems by Janet S. Wong (Simon & Schuster, 1994). Simple dramatic poems about growing up Asian American. Grades 3–5.

Echo and Narcissus

BACKGROUND

The story of Echo and Narcissus is a creation myth. Similar to the origin tale of Native America, the creation myth tells how something came to be. When they read Greek myths, students will find that all share the same pool of characters. Hera and Zeus, king and queen of the Olympian gods, are found in many tales, and even the minor deities and mortals are seen again and again.

Because this story is a Greek myth, our storyteller is assisted by a chorus. Choruses were used in traditional Greek plays as narrators who not only helped the story to move forward, but commented on the action as well.

STAGING TIPS

VOCABULARY

Narcissus (nar–SIS–us): A main character in the story; another name for daffodil; vanity.

Echo (EH–ko): A nymph and main character in the story. She is punished by Hera so that she can only repeat what others say.

Hera (heh–rah): Zeus' wife, Queen of the Gods.

Zeus (zoos): King of the Gods.

ambrosia (am–BROH–zhah): Known as "The Food of the Gods," it gives the gods immortality.

nymphs (nimfs): Minor female deities who rule over trees and flowers; sprightly.

When your students perform this play, have the chorus wear matching clothes and masks. Even something as simple as a half mask worn on the eyes and nose (feathered ones or Lone Ranger-type masks can be found at most drugstores or party stores) will give the chorus a feeling of unity. Other masks that are fun to make are paper-plate masks or, if you feel up to getting messy, try making plaster masks (see page 25).

Plaster Masks

MATERIALS

Rolls of plaster gauze (available at most drugstores)
Petroleum jelly
Scissors
String or elastic band
Tempera paint or markers
Fabric, glitter, or other decorative materials

WHAT TO DO

1. Have students wash their faces and tie back their hair. You may want to apply a small amount of petroleum jelly at the hairline to prevent the plaster from sticking to wispy pieces of hair.

2. Cut the plaster roll into strips about five inches long.

3. Follow the directions on the box of gauze to wet the plaster strips and mold them onto the students' faces. Be sure to leave air holes at the nostrils, mouth, and eyes. For students who are uncomfortable having their whole face covered, try doing only a portion of the face. Leave a hole at each side of the mask to attach a string or elastic band to make the mask easy to wear.

4. When the plaster dries, follow the directions on the box and remove the masks from the students' faces.

5. Have each student decorate his or her own mask with markers or tempera paint and small craft materials that can be glued on, like fabric and glitter.

Echo and Narcissus

◆ CHARACTERS ◆

The Storyteller	Chorus (three or more speakers)
Zeus	Hera
Echo	Narcissus

The Storyteller: Many folk tales around the world come from the myths that the Greeks and Romans told a long time ago. Myths were stories about the beliefs of the people who told them. The Greeks believed that gods who created the universe lived on Earth. Zeus was the king of all the gods, and Hera was his wife, the queen. Many myths showed how things in nature, like storms or mountains, were created by accident—often because the gods were up to mischief. In this myth we find out why we hear an echo, and how the narcissus flower was discovered.

Our story begins with Zeus standing in a wonderful wood speaking to a nymph whose name was Echo.

Chorus: And though she was beautiful, she loved to talk . . . a lot.

Zeus: Echo, I assume the feast of the wood nymphs is going ahead with no trouble.

Echo: Of course, Zeus. It's going to be great. We're going to have nuts and berries, and some ambrosia just for you, and Pan's going to play his flute. All the creatures of the woods will be there. Well, maybe not all of them . . .

Zeus: Echo, you must be quiet.

Echo: (*Whispering.*) Oh, don't worry Zeus. I'm really good at being quiet. Any time you need someone to shush or pipe down, I'm the nymph you should be looking for. All you have to do is tell me to be quiet and I'm like a wood mouse, or a wood-nymph mouse. Hee-hee. Oh, you know what I mean . . .

Zeus: Echo! I need you to be quiet because my wife, Hera, doesn't know I'm going to the wood nymph feast, and I need you to stand guard in case she comes into the woods.

Echo: Oh, I get it! You're being sneaky!

Zeus: Shhh!

Echo: (*Whispering.*) Oh, I get it! You're being sneaky!

Zeus: Right. I'm being sneaky. So if Hera shows up, tell her that you haven't seen me. Okay?

Echo: Okay, Zeus!

(*Zeus sneaks off one way while Hera enters from another. Echo keeps yelling after Zeus.*)

Echo: Don't worry about a thing! I'm not afraid of old Hera!

Hera: Ahem.

Echo: I'll just stand guard here!

Hera: Ahem!

Echo: Eek!

Hera: Who were you talking to, Echo?

Echo: Who me?

Hera: Yes, you. Who were you talking to?

Echo: I wasn't talking. That's so strange that you should say I was talking. I don't even like to talk. If you were to ask anybody what is one thing that Echo doesn't like to do, it would be talking. In fact, I even like doing laundry more than talking, and do you know how hard it is to find a good leaf detergent . . .

Hera: Be quiet! I am looking for my husband, Zeus.

Echo: I certainly haven't seen him. Zeus, you say. Hmmm. I don't even think I've ever heard of the guy. Nope, I don't even know my buddy Zeus.

Hera: Your buddy?

Echo: Oops.

Hera: You are lying to me. Now I'm going to have to punish you. So that you'll never lie again, I'll take away your ability to talk.

Echo: No. Please! Anything but that. I was making it up before about not liking to talk. I really do like to talk. In fact, it's my favorite thing in the world.

Hera: Okay, then I'll make it so that you can still talk, but you will only be able to say what other people say first.

(*She waves her hands as if casting a magic spell.*)

Echo: Other people say first.

Hera: You will repeat things, like a parrot.

Echo: Repeat things, like a parrot.

(*Echo can't believe what is happening.*)

Hera: That should teach you.

Echo: Should teach you.

Hera: Now where is that no-good husband of mine?

(Hera storms off as Echo tries to say something . . . anything. But every time she opens her mouth nothing will come out. Finally she begins to cry.)

Chorus Member 1: Echo was sad and hurt by the loss of her favorite activity.

Chorus Member 2: She probably would have sat there and cried for days if she hadn't heard the approach of the hunter Narcissus, a young man whom Echo was madly in love with.

Chorus Member 3: Narcissus was the most handsome man in all of the woods.

Chorus: She put aside her troubles for the moment and hoped to catch the hunter's attention.

(Narcissus enters with a bow and arrows. Echo stands to block his way.)

Narcissus: Well, hello.

Echo: Hello.

Narcissus: What can I do for you?

Echo: What can I do for you?

Narcissus: Well, wood nymph, you can let me pass so I can continue to hunt.

Echo: Continue to hunt.

(Echo is growing frustrated.)

Narcissus: Thank you.

Echo: Thank you.

(Narcissus attempts to pass, but Echo stands in his way again.)

Narcissus: Are you one of those wood nymphs who are in love with me because I am so handsome?

Echo: So handsome.

Narcissus: Yes, I am.

Echo: Yes, I am.

Narcissus: Not you, me!

Echo: Not you, me!

Narcissus: You are not as beautiful as I am. You're not good enough to love me.

Echo: (*Pleading.*) Love me.

Narcissus: Get out of my way, foolish nymph, before I strike you down!

Echo: Strike you down!

(*Narcissus angrily stalks off. Echo cries again and leaves.*)

Chorus Member 1: Echo was so upset by what had happened that she left the woods and went to live on a cliff on the side of a mountain all by herself.

Chorus Member 2: She lives there still and is so lonely without anyone to talk to that whenever anyone yells to her she responds, but she can still only say what that person has just said.

Chorus Member 3: Narcissus, on the other hand, was very proud of himself for how he acted, but, then again, he was always proud of himself.

Chorus: What he didn't know was that Hera had seen how he treated poor Echo.

Chorus Member 1: Even though Hera was the one who had punished Echo, she didn't want to see her suffer more just because of Narcissus' pride.

(*Hera enters into the woods. She waits for Narcissus, who enters soon after.*)

Hera: Hello there, Narcissus.

Narcissus: Great Queen Hera. You must have come to the woods to see my great beauty.

Hera: Of course I did, Narcissus. I've watched you hunt all day, and I thought you might need to rest and have a drink.

(She waves her hand and a fountain appears.)

Narcissus: Thank you, Hera. If you like, you can stay and watch me drink.

Hera: I have other things to attend to right now, but I'm sure I'll see you again. Good-bye.

Narcissus: That was strange that she wouldn't want to stay and look at me some more. Oh well, at least I have something to drink.

(He bends to drink from the fountain and sees his reflection.)

Narcissus: Well, would you look at that? There is a young man as good-looking as I am in there. Hello, handsome. Quiet sort of fellow. He must have come here just to look at me. He's so lucky to have someone who looks like me to look at. Yet he is so handsome himself. Perhaps I should stay and allow him to look. That way I can continue to look at him. Good idea, Narcissus. Brains and beauty.

(Narcissus stares into the fountain for a long time.)

Chorus Member 2: Narcissus was so in love with his own looks that he stood there for many years.

Chorus Member 3: As he stood there, he began to grow roots and became planted in the ground. Soon his body became a stem and his arms became leaves.

Chorus: And as a final punishment from Hera, his head became a yellow flower.

The Storyteller: So it seems that even though Hera took away Narcissus' life, she could not take away his beauty, and that is why the narcissus flower, which is also called a daffodil, is one of the most beautiful flowers of all.

Echo and Narcissus

ART AND WRITING
◆ Describing Fantastic Creatures

The myths of many countries present creatures that look very strange. Many of them are combinations of different animals (a lion with wings), while others take on attributes of the place they live (a volcano dweller made of fire). Have each student draw a fantasy creature that is a combination of his or her three favorite animals. To extend the activity, brainstorm different types of regional conditions, such as hot and desertlike or mountainous and snow-covered. Have each student pick one and draw what a fantastical being from that place might look like. Encourage the students to make their drawings as imaginative as they want.

Invite each student to write a descriptive paragraph about his or her mythical being. The descriptive words should be as vivid as possible. Challenge students to use adjectives to describe the features of their creatures (*razor-sharp eyes*) and adverbs coupled with powerful verbs to describe the creature's actions and abilities (*beats its wings powerfully*). Post the drawings around the room and have the students submit their paragraphs anonymously. Read the paragraphs out loud. Have the written details captured the visual ones accurately? If so, the class will be able to match the drawing with the description. If the class cannot guess, this is a great opportunity for fellow classmates to suggest ways to describe what they're seeing using vivid adjectives, clear nouns, and strong verbs.

THEATER ◆ Cooperative Acting

In the play, both Echo and Narcissus turn into something completely different from the people they were. One way this might be depicted is if several actors contribute to the new creation. For example, as Narcissus changes, the actor playing him can remain the same while another actor becomes his leaves, another his petals, and so on. An offstage actor can give Echo a repeated voice. How might the students use these techniques to turn a person into a bird, a tree, a car?

◆ RESOURCES ◆

Heroes, Gods and Monsters of Greek Myths by Bernard Evslin (Bantam Books,1987). Stories and illustrations of Greek mythology. Ages 9–12.

Further reading for teachers at www.bulfinch.org includes Greek myths from Thomas Bulfinch's *Mythology*.

The American Daffodil Society's Web site at www.daffodilusa.org provides beautiful pictures of daffodils (narcissus).

The Monkey and the Crocodile

BACKGROUND

Trickster tales are prevalent in many cultures. However, the form the trickster takes usually depends on the region itself. In many parts of Asia, the trickster is a monkey, an animal well suited to this role because of its quick-witted nature and ability to get itself out of sticky situations. In western Africa, Anansi the Spider is a clever creature, and many Native American groups have told stories about the cunning coyote. A number of tales by the Brothers Grimm fit into the trickster tale form and involve animals indigenous to Europe. This tale from India features the monkey, who faces another favorite folk tale animal, the crocodile.

VOCABULARY

cleverness
crocodile
wits
Ganges River (GAN–jeez)
carob

STAGING TIPS

The production of this play allows everybody to be wonderfully creative. Students can portray their characters with some simple masks and makeup. The journey through the water calls for clever staging ideas that can involve many students on stage (see Theater activity, page 41). In addition to having students play the part of the water, you can have them play the fruit trees—and even have several work together to play the crocodile. You might want to have the bulk of the story take place center stage in the water and let the sides of the stage serve as the islands to emphasize the distance between them. You could even have Baby Crocodile swim through the audience to create this effect.

Monkey Makeup

One of the major types of theatrical dance in India is called *Kathakali*. Here are instructions on how to create a "monkey" face by applying makeup Kathakali-style. (Of course, you can make your monkey look any way your imagination dictates by simply using your own colors and adding your own details.)

MATERIALS

Standard theatrical greasepaint in many colors. Greasepaint kits can be found in any costume/theatrical supply store and in most magic shops. Or you may find inexpensive face paint at a local drugstore (especially around Halloween time!).

Paintbrushes, makeup brushes, or cotton swab sticks for painting details

Makeup sponges for painting larger areas

WHAT TO DO

1. Load up a makeup sponge with dark green paint. Cover the outer edge of the face, leaving clear the areas around the eyes, nose, mouth and chin.

2. With a brush, paint the nose and cheeks in pink or red. Cover the lips in the same color.

3. Fill in the area around the mouth yellow.

4. To indicate a nose, paint an inverted triangle on the tip of the nose in purple or blue.

5. With a brush, put blue paint around the eyes. You can make the monkey's eyes big or small depending on how far you choose to extend the blue.

6. With a brush, use black to outline where one color meets another.

7. Use black to make eyebrows. These don't have to be where the natural eyebrows are but can be proportionate to the eyes you've drawn. What shape are the eyebrows? Is this monkey surprised? Happy? A little mean?

CLEANING UP

Most face paint will come off with soap and water, but double-check the instructions on the package to be sure that you do not need any specific type of makeup remover.

The Monkey and the Crocodile

◆ CHARACTERS ◆

The Storyteller   Baby Crocodile
Monkey   Mama Crocodile

The Storyteller: Trickster tales have always been a popular form of storytelling in most cultures. Trickster tales are stories about an animal or person who uses cleverness to get out of dangerous situations. Often it is that character's own cleverness that got him—or her!—into the situation in the first place. This story is a trickster tale that comes from India.

A long time ago, along the banks of the Ganges River in India, there lived a mama crocodile and her son.

Mama Crocodile: Son, have you finished your homework yet?

Baby Crocodile: (*From offstage.*) I'm just finishing up now, Ma.

Mama Crocodile: Well, come on in here, because I have a job for you to do.

(*Baby Crocodile enters.*)

Baby Crocodile: Sure, Ma, what can I do for you?

Mama Crocodile: I have a hankering for something delicious to eat.

Baby Crocodile: Do you want me to catch some fish for you?

Mama Crocodile: No. I'm tired of fish. I want a real treat for my dinner.

Baby Crocodile: What?

Mama Crocodile: I've never had one before, but I've heard that a monkey heart dinner is as good as it gets. I would like to taste one.

Baby Crocodile: A monkey heart? Gross!

(*Baby Crocodile makes a disgusted face.*)

Mama Crocodile: You don't have to eat it. But you do have to get it for me. Go and catch a monkey and bring it back here to me.

Baby Crocodile: Ma, monkeys live on land. They never go in the water.

Mama Crocodile: Yes, dear, that is correct.

Baby Crocodile: We live in the water, Ma, we never go on land.

Mama Crocodile: That is also correct.

Baby Crocodile: Well, Ma, if monkeys live on land and we live in the water, and they *never* come in the water and we *never* go on land, then how will I ever catch one?

Mama Crocodile: Well, dear, if you use your wits, you can find a way to trick a monkey into coming home with you. Now go, because I am already getting hungry.

The Storyteller: The crocodile went for a swim to think over his problem. As he was swimming, he passed a beautiful island full of locust trees.

Baby Crocodile: I can see the carob on the locust trees from here. Carob sure is sweet. If I had a sweet tooth, I would want some of that carob. It's too bad that monkeys can't swim across the river to get to it. They love sweets.

(*Baby Crocodile thinks for a minute. Suddenly he has an idea.*)

Baby Crocodile: Hey! That's how I can catch the monkey! I will offer him a ride across the river to get the carob. When he is trapped on my back in the middle of the river, I will swim home, and Mama can have her monkey heart dinner.

(*Baby Crocodile swims up to a monkey on the shore.*)

Baby Crocodile: Hi, Monkey! How are you?

Monkey: To tell you the truth, I am feeling kind of sad.

Baby Crocodile: Why?

Monkey: Coconuts. I've been eating coconuts for weeks. I wish there were something else around to have for dinner.

Baby Crocodile: Well, it's a good thing that I'm here. Can you see that island across the river? It's covered with locust trees full of sweet carob. Why don't you hop on my back, and I will swim you across the river to the island? Then you will be happy and full of yummy sweetness.

Monkey: Hmmm, I don't know about that, Crocodile. Crocodiles *eat* monkeys, you know.

Baby Crocodile: (*Makes a disgusted face.*) Gross. I don't eat monkeys.

Monkey: Really?

Baby Crocodile: Really. I prefer plain old fish.

Monkey: Still, how do I know you are telling the truth?

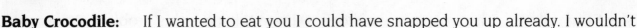

Baby Crocodile: If I wanted to eat you I could have snapped you up already. I wouldn't just sit here and *talk* to you.

Monkey: That's true. (*Monkey thinks it over for a moment.*) All right, let's go!

(*Monkey hops on Crocodile's back and they start swimming.*)

Baby Crocodile: This is great! I've never gone swimming with a monkey before!

Monkey: I've never gone swimming at all!

Baby Crocodile: My mama is going to love you!

Monkey: Your mother? Does she live on the island with the locust trees?

(*Baby Crocodile realizes his mistake and tries to cover it up.*)

Baby Crocodile: Um, well . . . she lives *near* it. That's it! She lives right near the island. Um, we probably have to pass right by her. Anyway, she will love you.

Monkey: Monkeys *are* lovable. We are a barrel of laughs. Do you want to hear a joke? What kind of key doesn't open doors?

Baby Crocodile: I don't know. What kind of key doesn't open doors?

Monkey: A mon-key! Ha! Ha! A monkey!

Baby Crocodile: You *are* funny! Do you know any other jokes?

Monkey: I know hundreds of jokes! Here's another one for you. What did the monkey do when someone stole his bananas? He went ape! Ha! He went ape! That is even funnier than the first joke!

Baby Crocodile: Ha! Ha! (*Pause.*) I don't get it.

Monkey: He went ape! (*Pause.*) Maybe it's only funny to monkeys.

Baby Crocodile: That's okay. I like you even if I don't understand all of your jokes. It's too bad that I have to bring you home to Ma for supper.

Monkey: Supper?!

Baby Crocodile: Oops. I mean, um—

Monkey: I thought you said that you don't eat monkeys.

Baby Crocodile: I don't. Mama does. She wants a monkey heart for supper. She told me to use my wits and trick a monkey into coming home with me. And you are no ordinary monkey. You tell jokes!

Monkey: Do you mean that your mama is going to eat my heart for supper?

Baby Crocodile: She's never tasted monkey heart before. She can't wait to try it.

Monkey: Oh. Well, I wish that you had told me this before you started swimming.

Baby Crocodile: Why?

Monkey: You don't think that I carry my heart wherever I go, do you? I have a heavy heart. I only bring it along when I know I will need it. Since you didn't mention it before we started swimming, I left my heart at home.

Baby Crocodile: Do you mean that you left your heart in that big tree on land? You don't have it with you right now? When I bring you to Mama, she won't be able to have your heart for supper?

Monkey: That's what I mean.

Baby Crocodile: This is awful! I told Ma that I would bring home a monkey so that she can have monkey heart for supper.

(*Crocodile starts to cry.*)

Monkey: Don't cry. Please, don't cry. I think that I can fix everything. Why don't you just swim back to land, and I will climb up the big tree and get my heart for you.

Baby Crocodile: Really?

Monkey: I would be happy to go back to my tree. I can't stand to see crocodile tears.

Baby Crocodile: Okay. Let's turn around.

The Storyteller: The monkey hopped off of the crocodile's back as soon as they got near land. He climbed up his tree as fast as he could. When he looked back down, the crocodile was waiting in the water for him.

Baby Crocodile: Monkey, please get your heart quickly. Ma must be very hungry by now.

Monkey: I have it!

Baby Crocodile: Great! Come down and bring it to me!

Monkey: I will throw it to you! Catch!

The Storyteller: The monkey stayed high up in his tree and threw a coconut down to the crocodile. Since neither the crocodile nor his mother had ever seen a real monkey heart, they didn't know the difference. Mama Crocodile spent all night working to get that coconut cracked open and then discovered that she didn't like it much after all. The monkey stayed in his tree laughing at what a trickster he  was until long past sundown. He never again tried to get carob from across the river and he enjoyed coconuts from that day on.

The Monkey and the Crocodile

SOCIAL STUDIES
◆ Studying Ecosystems

Each river supports a unique *ecosystem*, a group of life-forms that live in and around a place. Organize a class research project or simple fact hunt around river ecosystems. You might focus on a river related to the region of this play, like the Ganges River, the largest and most important river in India. Guide students with questions, such as *What do you think contributes to the type of animal and plant life that can survive near a river? Do you think that the same kinds of animals live near all rivers? What about the same kinds of plant life? What kind of plant and animal life is in the river closest to your home?* Students might create shoe box dioramas to show a specific ecosystem they've studied.

LANGUAGE ARTS
◆ Your Own Tricks

In this tale the crocodile was sneaky but got his comeuppance in the end, while the monkey was sneaky and used his wits to save his life. Have each student write a short personal narrative about a time that they were sneaky or played a trick on someone. How did it turn out in the end? Was playing a trick helpful, or did it cause trouble?

THEATER ◆ Creating Water

Think of how hard—and impractical!—it would be to use real water on stage to show a setting like the river in this play. Share with students one way to create the effect of water on stage: Stretch a blanket across the floor and have a few students grab the ends and move the material to make waves. Ask the students for other ideas to make water on stage. How could this be done with blue cellophane? Blue construction paper? How might a group of students dressed in blue create water with their bodies? What if just their hands were blue?

SCIENCE ◆ Predators

Discuss the meaning of the word *predator* with the class. Ask: *Who was the predator in this play. Who was the prey? What other animals have a predator/prey relationship?* Encourage students to research predators in different geographic regions. To show what they've learned, students can contribute predator-prey pairs to a class chart. You can easily turn this information into a Concentration-style card set by copying each predator-prey pair onto a pair of index cards. Use a different color marker for each pair so that students can verify a match.

◆ RESOURCES ◆

Ranger Rick Magazine at www.nwf.org/nwf/rrick contains articles about predators, wildlife, rivers, and more for kids of all ages.

The National Wildlife Federation homepage at www.nwf.org provides an informative site about nature for teachers.

Feet Water

BACKGROUND

Morality tales became popular throughout Europe during the Middle Ages. Most cultures have used morality tales to communicate their values and beliefs from one generation to the next. These stories have endured in many forms right up to the present. Morality tales such as "Little Red Riding Hood" and "Goldilocks and the Three Bears" are still popular and are told to remind our young ones of simple morals such as "don't talk to strangers" or "don't take what isn't yours." "Feet Water," a morality tale that originated in Ireland, reminds us of the importance of keeping your house and yourself clean.

VOCABULARY

cottages	linoleum
chores	superstitious
concerned	widow
routine	crumbs
continued	rage
delightful	spinning wheel
genius	feasted
situation	

Ireland, in particular, includes many fantastic creatures in its folklore. We have all heard tales of leprechauns, banshees, the Blarney stone, trolls, and gnomes, most of which are Irish in origin. This play contains such creatures as well. It employs the classic folk tale elements of inanimate objects coming to life (Feet Water) and supernatural beings (Spooks) in order to illustrate its moral.

STAGING TIPS

To effectively play this story in your classroom, you may want to use some common and fun theatrical conventions. Consider making Feet Water himself a puppet. A simple sock with eyes and some blue or gray strips of cloth glued to it can appear as a tub of water come to life. Because the spooks are otherworldly, they can look like anything you imagine (the wilder the better!). Paper-plate masks, simple makeup, or a decorated sheet can provide imaginative and fanciful ghosts. The spinning wheel and other household props can be easily mimed or cut from cardboard.

Feet Water

◆ **CHARACTERS** ◆

The Storyteller	Spook 1
Daughter	Spook 2
Mother	Feet Water

The Storyteller: *Top o' the mornin' to ya.* That's the way you say *good morning* in Ireland. I'm going to tell you a story that comes from Ireland. This kind of story is called a *morality tale*, which means that there is a moral, or a lesson to learn, at the end. Even though this story's moral is still important today, the story was written a long time ago—so long ago that the people of Ireland lived in stone cottages that had no floors.

Spook 1: No floors? That's silly. They would have fallen straight through the Earth.

The Storyteller: No. I mean that they had no wood or carpet or linoleum, only dirt.

Daughter: Dirt? Well, that must have been awfully messy. How could you ever know when it was clean?

The Storyteller: That was the reason it was so important to do all of your cleaning chores. Because you would want it to be as clean as it could possibly be.

Mother: But even if you swept the entire floor, your feet would still be dirty.

The Storyteller: That's why every house had a tub that they used just for cleaning their feet at the end of the day, before they went to bed. The old people of the village were very superstitious. And one of the warnings they gave was that you should never keep feet water in the house overnight, or a bad thing might come in.

Spook 1: (*Whispering.*) Besides, feet water must stink really bad.

The Storyteller: Of course it did. But I think they were more concerned with a bad thing coming into the house.

Spook 2: (*Whispering.*) What kind of bad thing?

The Storyteller: I think we're going to find out. The only things we need now are the people who live in this cottage.

Mother and Daughter: Here we are.

The Storyteller: Then let's begin. A long time ago, there lived a widow and her daughter. Every night they would eat supper together, and after they were finished they would always clean up. First, they would put away the leftover food and clean up the crumbs on the table. Then, they would sweep the dirt floor to make sure that they cleaned up any leaves or grass or loose dirt. Finally, they brushed their teeth and washed their feet in the tub they had just for that purpose.

(*Mother and Daughter both wash their feet.*)

The Storyteller: They would always take turns throwing out the feet water each night.

Mother: Wait! Before we throw out the feet water, we should be kind to any animals that might be resting outside the window.

The Storyteller: Okay, then. We'll yell, "Look out below!" and throw the feet water out the window.

All: Look out below!

(They throw out the feet water. Then move back to their places with a "Whew.")

The Storyteller: After the widow and her daughter threw out the feet water, they would go to bed. Every night this was the routine they followed. There was, however, one night when they didn't follow it. You see, sometimes in Ireland the wind blows strong and the rain pours so hard that you might swear someone was pounding on your rooftop. This was one of those nights.

Mother: Daughter, it's so cold tonight. Why don't we just wash our feet and crawl into bed?

Daughter: You mean I don't have to put away the leftover food from supper and clean up all the crumbs, or sweep the floor of all the leaves and loose dirt? Or throw out the feet water?

Mother: Not tonight, dear.

The Storyteller: And with that, the widow and her daughter washed their feet and went to bed. The storm continued to rage on through the night. But the widow and her daughter were safe and cozy in their warm, but dirty, cottage until . . .

(A slow foreboding knock is heard at the door.)

Daughter: Mother, I didn't like the sound of that knock. Who is it?

(There is no answer.)

Mother: Oh, well. It must have been the wind.

Spooks: Feet Water, Feet Water, let us in.

(Feet Water jumps from the tub.)

Feet Water: Oh, yeah! Who's calling me?

Spooks: Feet Water, Feet Water, let us in.

Feet Water: What do they mean *in*? Oh, wow. I'm inside. I never get to stay in the cottage overnight. I guess I have the splash of the place. Hmm. What should I do first?

Spooks: Oh, Feet Water.

Feet Water: Oh, yeah. Those guys outside, whoever they are. Well, this is the first time I've been left inside overnight. I'm going to do whatever I want. Ha-ha. Let's just see who this is.

(*Feet Water hops out of the tub and opens the door. Spooks enter.*)

Spook 1: What a terrible night to be outside. Thank you for letting us in, Feet Water.

Feet Water: Hey, you guys don't have to thank me. I figure if these folks are going to let me stay in here, we can have a party here every night.

Spook 2: As delightful as that sounds, we are simply seeking a place to sit and work.

(*Spook 1 sets the spinning wheel down and Spook 2 sits and starts spinning yarn.*)

Feet Water: You guys are no fun. Why did I even let you in? I'll be over here in the tub if you want to cause any trouble. Heh-heh.

The Storyteller: The widow and her daughter were so scared that they just pulled the covers up over their faces. The spooks stayed for hours and did their spinning until . . .

Spook 2:   I'm getting hungry. But I don't want to go back out into a stormy night.

Spook 1:   Maybe we can get Feet Water to go out and get us something to eat.

Feet Water: Hold it. Hold everything. If you think I'm going outside, so that I can get locked out, or get washed down some drain, you are sadly mistaken.

Spook 1:   But we're hungry.

Feet Water: Hungry, schmungry. I'm staying put.

Spook 2:   Well then, we're going to have to go out to find some food.

Feet Water: Wait a minute. Look at this in the kitchen. They didn't clean up after their supper.

Spook 1:   We need food, not trash.

Feet Water: But it is food. They didn't put away their bread after they ate tonight. You can stay here and eat their leftovers.

Spook 2:   Feet Water, you're a genius.

(*Spooks start to eat the bread. Feet Water goes back to the tub and waits.*)

The Storyteller: So, as you can see, the spooks were able to stay and eat the leftovers that the widow and her daughter didn't clean up that night. They feasted for a long time, and so quietly that the widow and her daughter were sure they must have left the cottage.

Daughter: Mother? Do you think they're gone?

Mother: Earlier I heard them say they would have to go out and get some food.

Daughter: Yes. I heard them say that, too. And now I don't hear them at all.

Mother: You're right, Daughter. They must have gone.

(*They are surprised to see that the spooks are still there, and they jump back under the covers.*)

Daughter: Mother? Why are they still here?

Mother: I don't know, daughter . . . Oh, no. We left the bread out. I'm afraid we've made a terrible mistake by not cleaning up after supper. From now on we shall always put away our leftovers.

Daughter: Agreed, Mother.

Spook 1:   I'm full, so we can get back to work.

(*Spooks go back to their spinning wheel.*)

Mother: Daughter, now is our chance. If we clean up our leftovers they will leave for sure.

Daughter: Good idea, Mother.

(*Mother and Daughter clean up the leftovers.*)

The Storyteller: The widow and her daughter were sure that the spooks would grow hungry again, and now that they had put away all the food, would have to leave the cottage. So they got back into bed and waited, but hunger was not the next thing on the spooks' minds.

Spook 1:   I'm getting tired. Can we take a break?

Spook 2:   We deserve a rest. But I think we have a problem here. No place to lie down.

Spook 1:   There are only two beds and they are already taken.

Spook 2:   I'd really hate to have to leave now. Our work is almost finished, and it is still raining.

Daughter: Did you hear that, Mother? They can see that there's no place else to sleep, so now they'll leave for sure.

Spook 2:   I've got it. Oh, Feet Water!

Feet Water: Oh, yeah! How can I be of service?

Spook 1:   Feet Water, we need a place to rest for a while, but the only two beds are taken.

Feet Water: If I want to lie down, I just splash down here on the floor.

Spook 2:   We need something a bit more comfortable than that.

Feet Water: Look at this floor. Those two messy people didn't even sweep the floor. Look at all the dirt, and grass, and loose leaves. You can make some little beds and pillows out of all that—you'll be plenty comfy.

Spook 2:   Oh, Feet Water, you are a genius.

Mother: Daughter? Did you hear that?

Daughter: Yes, Mother.

Mother: If they get some rest, they'll probably stay for two days. Now I really think leaving the house a mess was a bad idea.

Mother and Daughter: Oh, dear!

The Storyteller: The spooks started to make beds out of the dirt, and grass, and leaves when the daughter decided that she wouldn't be scared anymore, and came up with an idea.

Daughter: Mother, I've got it. If being messy got us into this situation, then cleaning up will get us out. (*Gets out of bed.*) Attention, everybody! We understand that you're going to need a place to sleep. My mother and I would love to help you out and make the beds on the floor for you.

Spooks: Really? You'd do that for us?

Daughter: Oh, sure. You go and relax, and your beds will be ready in a jiffy. (*To Mother.*) Now is our chance to clean up so they'll go away.

Mother: Oh, Daughter, that's such a good idea.

(*Mother and Daughter clean the cottage.*)

Daughter: There. Now the cottage is clean again.

Spook 2:   Hey, you promised to make us some beds, so where are they?

Daughter: Well, as you can see, there is no dirt, or grass, or leaves to make any beds out of.

Spook 1:   So Feet Water was wrong. What do we do now?

Spook 2:   As far as I can see, we have no choice but to find a new place to do our spinning.

Spooks: Awwww.

(*Spooks start to pick up their spinning equipment when Feet Water pops up from his bucket.*)

Feet Water: Hey. Whoa. Wait just a minute here. Where are you going?

Spook 1:   You tricked us, Feet Water. You said there would be enough dirt, or grass, or leaves to make some beds. But you can see that there isn't. So now we are just going to have to leave.

(*They leave.*)

Mother: Oh, my Daughter. That was wonderful. How did you think of that?

Daughter: Well, at first I was really glad that I didn't have to clean up after supper tonight, but even as I was going to sleep, I couldn't help but think we should have cleaned up all along.

Mother: And now the cottage is clean again, and nothing bad will happen. Thank you so much for getting rid of those spooks. We will never again go to bed without doing our chores.

(*They go back to bed very satisfied. Moments later we hear a knock on the door. Mother and Daughter sit upright, scared and confused. Feet Water pokes his head up.*)

Mother: Daughter, we forgot to get rid of the feet water.

(*Mother and Daughter lunge for the bucket.*)

Spooks: Feet Water, Feet Water, let us in.

Feet Water: Oh, yeah!

Mother: Oh, no. Not this time, you don't!

Feet Water: Wait a minute. What are you doing? I won't cause any trouble, I promise. I'll just sit in the tub quietly. I have to catch up on some reading anyway.

All: Look out below!

(They throw Feet Water away. Mother and Daughter hug each other.)

The Storyteller: With Feet Water out of the house, the strange beings went away for good.

(Mother and Daughter go back to bed.)

The Storyteller: Now, I'm sure that there is a floor in your house or apartment. And I'm sure that throwing away some nasty feet water isn't part of your evening chores. And I'm not so superstitious myself to think that if you don't clean up before bed, something bad will happen. But I will say this: After I heard this story, I decided, just like the widow and her daughter, that I would never again go to bed without making sure that my house and my self are nice and neat and clean.

All: The end.

Feet Water

SOCIAL STUDIES ◆ *Superstitions*

Discuss what a superstition is. What Irish superstition is played out in "Feet Water"? What other superstitions have the students heard of? Do they think that superstitions differ from country to country? City to city? Why or why not?

LANGUAGE ARTS ◆ *Other Worlds*

The story itself never explains exactly where the spooks came from or why they need to spin yarn. Using the information given in the play, have the students imagine what the world of the spooks might be like. Students can show their creative thinking by writing an interview with one of the spooks. Help students organize their ideas by brainstorming possible interview questions to ask the spooks. Some possible questions include: *What does your world look like? Why did you go to that particular house? What other creatures inhabit the world where you live? Why do you spin and what do you do with all of the yarn?* Students should write the questions down and then answer the questions from the spooks' point of view. Read the interviews out loud. Compare and contrast them to illustrate the diversity of ideas that came up.

THEATER ◆ *Puppet Voices*

A fun way to stage this play might be to make the character of Feet Water a puppet. To help give life and voice to a tub of water, try this game that will facilitate creativity and critical thinking. Have two students sit in chairs at the front of the room. Suggest a simple topic for them to discuss, such as what has happened in school today, and assign each student an inanimate object to portray, such as an apple or a pencil. Ask them to have a conversation using a voice they think their object might speak in. Remind them that there are no wrong responses in this game and that what they say isn't important, only the voice they use to say it.

By practicing giving voices to many different objects, students will exercise their creative muscles (find a voice that is fun for them) and improve their critical-thinking skills (make a correlation between what an object looks like or is used for and what it might sound like). This exercise will also build students' confidence and provide a clearer understanding of how to find a voice for the character of Feet Water, should you decide to stage the play in class.

◆ RESOURCES ◆

Little Book of Irish Superstitions by Kim Lenaghan (Appletree Press, 1999).

Find a list of Irish superstitions at Irish Eye's "Superstions" page at www.mindmills.net/irisheyes/supersti tions. html (for teachers). Family Play's activity pages offer easy-to-follow directions for making puppets with everyday materials (perfect for upper-elementary students, though suggested ages are younger) at www.familyplay.com/activities/actPuppets.html.

Tangled-up Feet

BACKGROUND

As the storyteller states in the introduction, most regions of the world have stories about foolish people. Many countries have tales about an entire town of foolish people. In Jewish folklore that town is called Chelm, in England it is Gotham, and in Mexico, where this next story is from, it is a village called Lagos. Some of the stories teach other, minor lessons, but the main moral is usually "don't act foolishly." These fool's tales (as they are called) are greatly entertaining, and variations on them continue to be a source of humor in books, plays, and films. Many fool's tales have changed over time to become the jokes that everyone knows and that children continue to tell in the schoolyard.

VOCABULARY

vaquero (va-KER-o): Spanish for "cowboy" or "drover."

mi amiga(o): Spanish for "my friend." An *a* at the end of the word means the friend is female, an *o* means the friend is male.

cattle

genius

You may also want to briefly explain the role of the vaquero in Mexico and the cowboy in the southwestern United States: primarily to take mature cattle to the marketplace. In the days before railroads and trucks, this had to be done on horseback, by supervising the cattle as they walked routes often hundreds of miles long.

STAGING TIPS

To produce this play on the stage, the students may want to review traditional vaquero costumes and dress the four vaqueros similarly, perhaps with a different color kerchief or hatband for each. You may also want to explore and heighten the idea of the tangled-up feet by having the students playing the vaqueros wear grossly oversized shoes.

Tangled-up Feet

◆ CHARACTERS ◆

The Storyteller	Girl
The Four Vaqueros:	
Pablo	Pedro
Pancho	Earl

The Storyteller: Most countries have stories about foolish people. Many countries have tales about an entire town of foolish people. In Mexico, that town is a village called Lagos. And Lagos is where our story takes place. As hard as they try, the people of Lagos are never able to find an easy solution to their problems.

This fool's tale is about four vaqueros. *Vaquero* is a Spanish word for *cowboy*, someone who rides a horse and helps move herds of cattle from one place to another. These four vaqueros were about to finish a hard day's work, but they had a problem.

(Pancho, Pablo, Pedro, and Earl enter. Earl is looking for a lost cow.)

Earl: Here, cow, cow, cow. Come back, Fluffy!

Pablo: You might as well stop looking. I think he is gone for good.

Earl: I have to find him! He's my favorite cow! Fluffy! Arf! Arf!

Pedro: Earl, cows don't "arf."

Earl: This one does. Pancho taught him to speak dog.

Pancho: I tried to teach him cow, but he wasn't any good at it.

Earl: Fluffy! Where are you?

Pablo: I've got it! Earl, maybe he is hiding behind you.

Earl: Pablo, you are a genius! I'll look behind me.

(Earl begins to spin in circles like a dog chasing its tail.)

Earl: He's not hiding behind me. Is he behind you, Pancho?

Pancho: (Starts spinning.) Nope. Nope. He's not behind me, either.

Pedro: Is he behind you, Pablo?

Pablo: I don't know. Is he behind you, Pedro?

(Pedro and Pablo start to spin around. After some time they all stop and are very dizzy.)

Earl: I'm dizzy.

Pablo: I am, too. Let's sit down for a few minutes and rest.

The Storyteller: The vaqueros all leaned against a big tree and plopped right down on the ground and fell asleep. They slept for a long time. When they woke up, the cow had not returned, but they realized that they had an even bigger problem.

(The vaqueros yawn and stretch.)

Pablo: Time to get back to work.

(They try to get up, but their feet are tangled together in a pile. They cannot get up. They try again, but still cannot get up.)

Pedro: What's wrong with our feet?

Pancho: I can't tell which ones are mine.

Pancho: What are we going to do?

Pedro: We will be stuck here forever if we don't find our own feet.

Earl: *(Crying.)* I miss Fluffy and now I miss my little piggies. *(Points to toes.)*

Pancho: Which ones?

Earl: *(Crying.)* The one that had roast beef, and the one that went to market . . .

Pablo: I've got it! Let's yell for help.

Pancho: Pablo, you're a genius! Let's yell for help. Help! Help!

(They all begin to yell for help. No help arrives. They stop yelling and sigh.)

Pedro: That didn't work. Now what are we going to do?

Pablo: I've got another idea! What is the best way to get something that you want?

Pancho: Ask for it.

Pablo: Right. Let's ask our feet to untangle.

Pedro: Pablo, you are a genius! Let's have a talk with our toes.

Earl: Excuse me, little piggy, are you listening?

(There is no answer.)

Pedro: Hello! Feet! Will you please untangle?

(Girl with a basket enters and stands quietly next to the vaqueros. The vaqueros do not notice her. They all begin to ask their feet to untangle. They stop asking and sigh.)

Pancho: I don't think my feet are speaking to me. We had an argument last week and they are still mad.

Pedro: Nothing is working.

Earl: What are we going to do? I don't want to stay here all night!

Pablo: I've got it! Let's yell for help.

Pancho: Pablo, you're a genius! Let's try yelling for help. Help! Help!

(*They all yell for help again. Earl sees the girl and speaks to her.*)

Earl: Excuse me, would you please yell for help with us?

Girl: Why are you yelling for help?

(*They all stop and look at the girl as if she must be foolish.*)

Pancho: Um . . . Mi amiga, open your eyes. Can't you see our problem? Look right here. (*Points to feet.*)

Pablo: Our feet are tangled up.

Pedro: They won't tell us which of them belongs to which of us.

Girl: I think I can help you.

Pablo: Good. Please go into Lagos, where we are from, and tell our wives and children that we are stuck here and will never be able to get home again.

Earl: (*Crying.*) I miss home, and the piggy that went wee, wee, wee . . .

Girl: I don't need to go to Lagos. I can help you untangle your feet.

Pedro: Really? How will you do that?

Girl: Well, I see one pair of blue shoes. Whoever wears blue shoes owns that pair of feet. Which one of you put on blue shoes this morning?

Pablo: I think I did . . . no, maybe that was yesterday.

Pedro: I had blue shoes when I was just a boy.

Earl: I like the color blue.

Girl: I can tell this is getting us nowhere. Look, on this foot here, the big toe is poking right out for all to see. Now which one of you can feel a draft on his big toe?

Pancho: I feel a draft on my head. Maybe my shoe is a hat.

Earl: What's a draft?

Girl: Forget it. I have a better idea. (*She reaches into her basket and pulls out a long knitting needle. She pokes one of the feet with the needle.*)

Earl: Ouch! What did you do that for?

(*She pokes Earl again.*)

Earl: Ouch!

Girl: That one is your foot. (*She pokes another foot.*)

Pancho: Ouch!

Girl: That one is yours.

(*She continues to poke their feet as they begin to untangle themselves. They finally all stand up.*)

Pablo: Thank you for helping us. Who knows how long we would have been stuck there if you hadn't come along?

Earl: Now we can go back to looking for Fluffy.

Girl: Fluffy?

Pablo: Earl's cow.

Girl: Oh.

Earl: Here, Fluffy! Arf! Arf!

Girl: Cows don't "arf."

Pancho: This one does. I taught him to speak dog.

(The men all begin "arfing" and looking for the cow.)

Girl: I sure hope I never act that foolish.

(Girl watches for a moment, then shrugs her shoulders and joins in.)

Tangled-up Feet

SOCIAL STUDIES ◆ *In Other Words*

This play introduced some Spanish words, like *mi amiga* and *vaqueros*. Ask students to expand their vocabularies by introducing words related to the play in other languages they speak besides English. Ask: *How do you say* my friend *in other languages? How many languages have a word for* cowboy? *How do people in your family who speak a language besides English say* hello? You and your students can begin an ongoing class chart with a few words that can serve as catalysts for language exploration.

LANGUAGE ARTS ◆ *Many Fools*

We have all read books or seen movies about foolish people. Encourage students to brainstorm other familiar characters who are foolish or backward, such as Amelia Bedelia or the people of Chelm, and list some of the foolish things they do.

As a class, map out a story outline. Choose one of the foolish characters and make a list of three or four problems he or she might find himself or herself having. Next to each problem, write several foolish ways this character might try to "solve" the problem. Use this class story map as a model for students to create their own foolish characters and make a story plan. Invite students to write their stories or record them on audiotape.

THEATER ◆ *Portraying Real Life*

In this play the characters experience some very common feelings. How might students show that their characters are sad, hungry, thirsty, frustrated, or confused? What actions can best depict these feelings? How might *tired* be different from *exhausted*?

A fun way to practice expressing characters' emotions—and build vocabulary—is to play a game of charades in which you give a student an emotion to act out for the rest of the class. The first student to correctly guess the emotion (and, for advanced students, to also give a synonym or antonym for the emotion) gets to act out the next emotion.

MATH ◆ *Word Problems*

Have students invent some word problems based on the characters in the play. Post them as word problems of the day. Here are some examples to get you started:

❖ If all four vaqueros were barefoot when their feet got tangled up, how many toes would you see?

❖ If each vaquero, except Earl, has six cows, and Earl has two plus Fluffy, how many cows do they have all together?

◆ RESOURCES ◆

Vaqueros: America's First Cowmen by Martin W. Sandler (Holt, 2000).

Buckaroos in Paradise at http://rs6.loc.gov/ammem/ncrhtml/crview00.html provides information for teachers about the history of vaqueros in the western U.S. and Mexico.

Photojournalist Jeffrey Scott's photographs of modern vaqueros can be found at www.azstarnet.com/~jeffoto/vaqueros.html.

How Man Got Fire

BACKGROUND

Many cultures have developed *origin tales* to explain natural phenomena. In the origin tales of Native American cultures, it is most often an animal that is responsible for creating or delivering something, as in this tale where Fox delivers fire to man. In this way, origin tales differ from myths, which usually rely on the interference of the gods to create the natural event. Take, for example, the story of Narcissus and Echo (page 24), in which an echo is created because the goddess Hera punishes a talkative wood nymph. Origin tales, instead, rely on the cunning and cleverness of the story's hero to aid in the creation. While most tales of this sort have in common the presence of animals, the details reflect the region and culture from which the tale originated. Folk legends of the Apache, from the southwest region of the United States (see map, page 71), often characterize the fox as the cleverest of all animals, while groups from other areas have their own cast of characters. Across Native American cultures, however, the origin tale always serves the same purpose.

VOCABULARY

Apache	cleverest
greediest	accidentally
interesting	ridiculous
delicious	frightened
brilliantly	roaring bonfire
panicked	constructed
surrounded	temporarily
gathered	juniper berries
decorated	drought
catapulted	ember
nurturing	

STAGING TIPS

Consider creating the fireflies as shadow puppets. Cut them out of cardboard and put them on sticks. Put up a screen (a big white sheet stretched taut works well) and light it from behind. Have students "fly" the fireflies behind the screen. When the light is on, the audience will be able to see them, and when it is off they will not. You can also make smaller shadow puppets and attach them to pipe cleaners or thin wire. Instead of using a backlit screen, put the puppets on an overhead projector and use the wire or pipe cleaner as a stick to move them around. You might also try using pin flashlights to represent the bugs. The students speaking for the flies can blink their light when their fly is speaking.

How Man Got Fire

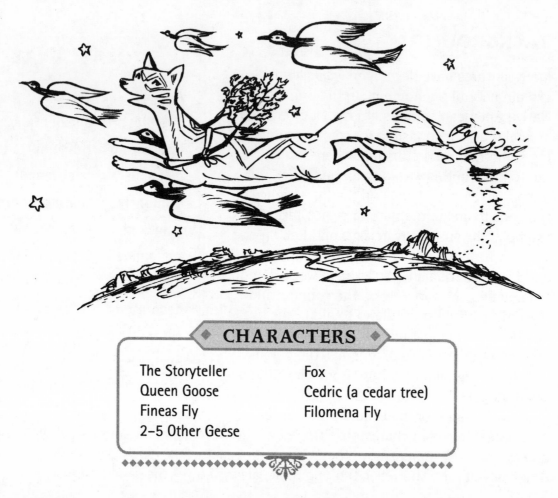

◆ CHARACTERS ◆

The Storyteller
Queen Goose
Fineas Fly
2–5 Other Geese

Fox
Cedric (a cedar tree)
Filomena Fly

The Storyteller: Many folk tales are about how things came to be, such as why certain animals look the way they do, or how certain things in nature changed over time. Native Americans have a very rich history of these tales and have passed them down from generation to generation to explain the way they lived.

This story comes from the Apache who lived in what is now the southwestern United States. They believed that the fox was the cleverest and the greediest of all animals. They also believed in the *Ga'ns*, protective mountain spirits who watched over them. And they believed that many years ago the all the animals and trees used to talk to each other, and that before man had fire, the only animals to have it were the fireflies. Because the fox was the cleverest and the greediest of the animals, he accidentally helped man get fire.

(Geese fly over Fox's head, honking wildly. Fox watches them.)

Fox: That's an interesting sound.

(Honking continues.)

Fox: Here I am, Fox, the cleverest of all the animals, and I don't have a sound nearly as interesting as that one. I must learn to honk like that. Oh, Geese! Geese! Down here!

(The geese see Fox on the ground and land to meet him.)

Queen Goose: Yes, Mr. Fox, what can we do for you?

Fox: Today you may teach me how to honk.

Queen Goose: A honking fox. What a ridiculous idea.

All Other Geese: Yes, how silly.

(All the geese honk in agreement.)

Fox: You will teach me how to honk, or I will imagine myself having a delicious goose feast *very* soon.

Queen Goose: Very well, then, we will teach you how to honk. But we can't do it here.

All Other Geese: No, not here.

Fox: Why not?

Queen Goose: Well, Mr. Fox, everybody knows that geese do their best honking while they are in the air. If you want to learn how to honk like some of the all-time great honking geese, you must come fly with us.

All Other Geese: Yes, come fly with us!

(*All the geese honk in agreement.*)

Fox: Gulp! Me? Fly? But . . .

Queen Goose: Oh, don't you worry, Mr. Fox. We will make wings for you and carry you through the sky. But you must remember the most important rule of flying.

Fox: What's that?

All Geese: Don't look down.

Storyteller: The geese flew to find the fullest branches on the trees and constructed some wings for the fox. They then grabbed hold of the new wings, and with fox holding on tight, took off into the evening sky, honking away.

(*Geese all honk.*)

Fox: Yahoo!

Queen Goose: Remember, Mr. Fox, don't look down. In fact, you may want to close your eyes while we are in the air.

Fox: I already have them closed. How high up are we?

Queen Goose: Well, we are higher than any trees, even higher than the mountains.

Fox: Whoa!

(*All the geese honk. Fox holds on even tighter and looks scared.*)

The Storyteller: Fox was so frightened at being so high off the ground that he didn't even remember to listen to the honking that the geese were doing. He just held on and kept his eyes shut as tight as they could be. Soon the geese flew over the village of the fireflies, which was brilliantly lit up by the roaring bonfire they kept burning in the center all the time.

Fox: I can tell there is some light. We must have reached the sun.

Queen Goose: We haven't reached the sun.

Fox: Then we must have been flying all night. It must be morning.

All Other Geese: It isn't morning.

Fox: But that light is so bright, I must see what it is.

The Storyteller: Fox opened his eyes and saw how high up he was, and he panicked.

Fox: Ahhhhh!!!!!!

Queen Goose: I told you not to open your eyes.

(All *the geese honk. Fox struggles and lets go of the wings.*)

The Storyteller: Down he went. Past the clouds and toward the bright light he had seen through his closed eyelids. With a splash, he landed in a puddle inside the walled village of the fireflies.

Fineas Fly: Wow! That's the biggest firefly I've ever seen.

Filomena Fly: Oh, the poor thing. His fire went out.

Fox: I am not a firefly. I am Fox, the cleverest of all the animals.

Fineas Fly: Well, you weren't clever enough not to fall out of the sky, were you?

Filomena Fly: I've never heard of a fox.

Fineas Fly: I haven't either. What kind of bug is a fox?

Fox: I am not a bug at all.

Filomena Fly: Then how did you get here? The whole village is surrounded by tall cedar trees so that nothing that crawls can come in, only bugs and birds that fly.

Fox: Well, I flew temporarily.

Fineas and Filomena:	Ohhh.
Fox:	I need to find a way back to where I came from.
Fineas Fly:	But the only way out of here is the way you came in. And you have no wings.
Filomena Fly:	But don't worry, you can stay here with us.
The Storyteller:	The fireflies led Fox to the center of the village where the fireflies gathered around the fire, which burned brighter than ever. Fox had never seen anything so beautiful, other than the sun itself, and he decided that he should have the fire for himself. So he devised a plan.
Fox:	Fireflies one and all! In order to thank you for the great kindness you have shown me by treating me as one of your own, I wish to throw the greatest festival the fireflies have ever seen.

(*The fireflies cheer.*)

Fox:	If you allow me to go to the edge of the village and prepare, I will come back with gifts that we can all share, and enjoy ourselves well into the night.

(*The fireflies cheer again as Fox heads toward the edge of the village.*)

The Storyteller:	The fox went to the edge of the village and found wood to make drums, the first drums anyone had ever seen or heard. He also found juniper berries to make necklaces for the fireflies, and some white clay with which he decorated himself. Oh, and one other thing: Fox tied a branch to his tail. Then he went back to the center of the village.
Fineas Fly:	Hooray for Fox! I love a party!
Filomena Fly:	Hooray for Fox! This will be the best night ever!

The Storyteller: The fireflies got dressed up in the necklaces that Fox had made, and they jumped up and down on the drums, and they danced in a circle around the fire.

(The geese honk overhead.)

Fox: *(To himself.)* There are the geese again. Now's my chance.

(Fox dances so that the branch that is tied to his tail rests in the fire. The geese honk even louder overhead.)

Fox: *(To himself.)* I must be quick. *(To the fireflies.)* Boy, it sure is warm dancing around this fire. I don't know how you fireflies can even stand it.

Filomena Fly: Of course you're warm; you're wearing a fur coat.

Fox: If you'll excuse me, I'm going to go rest a minute at the edge of the village.

(Fox runs off. The geese honk even louder overhead.)

The Storyteller: Faster than it takes the light from a firefly's tail to disappear, Fox had run away with the fire attached to his own tail. The surprised fireflies tried to catch him, but Fox was one of the fastest runners in the world, and the fireflies could not fly fast enough to overtake him. He ran all the way to the cedar trees that surrounded the village.

Fox: Cedar tree! Hey, cedar tree!

Cedric: Hay is for horses, and we don't grow any of that here. If you wish to address me, my name is Cedric.

Fox: I'm sorry, Cedric. I have something for you.

Cedric: Oh, sure. Where were you last month when there was a drought, and I needed a little water?

(The geese honk very loudly now. They are directly overhead.)

Fox: Please, Cedric, bend down to me. I want to hang colored shells in your bough.

Cedric: Oh, you *do* have something for me.

The Storyteller: I don't want you to think badly about old Cedric—usually trees aren't that easy to fool—but Fox was clever, and he climbed on the top of the tree when Cedric bent down.

Cedric: Get off of me. What do you think you're doing?

Fox: I think I'll sit here as long as I want.

Cedric: I know how to get you off.

The Storyteller: With that, Cedric stood up straight as quickly as he could and catapulted Fox high up into the air. Of course that was all part of Fox's plan, because just then the geese were making their way back over the village, and Fox grabbed on to Queen Goose's legs.

Queen Goose: My word. I believe we've found Mr. Fox again. And he has fire attached to his tail.

Fox: Keep flying, Queen Goose. It's time I went home again.

(The geese fly and Fox keeps his eyes closed.)

The Storyteller: What Fox didn't realize is that fire burns, and as he flew, that branch that was attached to his tail burned away and scattered fire all over the land. By the time he got to his burrow there was only one small ember left. And the fireflies had finally caught up to him.

(Fineas and Filomena take back the ember attached to Fox's tail.)

Fineas Fly: Now we're going to have to spend so much time nurturing this fire back to what it was.

Filomena Fly: You are a bad, bad fox. Your punishment for stealing our fire is that you will never be able to use fire for yourself.

The Storyteller: And never again did the Fox use fire. But what about all the fire that fell to the ground on his flight? That fire was found by the Apache people. Soon they learned to use it for themselves to cook their food and keep themselves warm through the cold winters.

How Man Got Fire

SOCIAL STUDIES
◆ Exploring Cultures

This story came from the Apache, who lived in the southwest region of North America. Have students use the map on page 71 to figure out how the story might change if it were told by a Native American group from a different region. For example, what animals might be in the story if it were told by the Cree (subarctic region)? What type of climate, animals, and setting details might the Chinook (northwest region) use in their stories? What Native American groups come from the area you live in and how might their stories be different?

READING ◆ Origin Tale
Compare-and-Contrast Chart

Offer students a selection of other origin tales and have them choose several to read. In small groups or individually, students can compare the structure of these origin stories to "How Man Got Fire." Provide or work with the class to develop a chart in which they can detail the similarities and differences among animal characters, natural phenomena, setting details, problems, and other story structure points.

THEATER ◆ Animal Images

All of the characters in the play are animals. Have the students try different facial expressions to play each of the animals. Ask them to name some other animals and see how those might be played. Generate more ideas with questions, like *How would the animals walk? How would they talk? How might you change the your expression so that you look like that?* Have the students pick their favorite animals and act like them. How might some of these animals interact?

SCIENCE ◆ The Real Story of Fire

This play tells how fire was given to man. How much do the students know about the science behind fire? Do they know what causes it or how to make it? Why do matches light? What causes lightning? Why do fireflies light up? Use this story as a bridge to a science lesson about fire, heat and lightning (see Resources).

◆ RESOURCES ◆

The Apache Indians by Nicole Claro (Chelsea House, 1993) examines the history, culture, and future prospects of the Apache. Ages 9–12.

From Sea to Shining Sea: A Treasury of American Folklore and Folk Songs compiled by Amy L. Cohn (Scholastic, 1993). A multicultural anthology of stories, songs, and other American folk literature, including Native American myths.

Smokey Bear at www.smokeybear.com provides information about forest fires and fire prevention.

Native American Cultures by Region

Arctic: Inuit, Yuit, and Aleut

Subarctic: Cree, Chippewa, Montagnais, Naskapi, Chipewyan, Beaver, Kutchin, Tanana

Northwest Coast: Tlingit, Tsimshian, Haida, Kwakiutl, Nootka, Chinook, Tillamook

Plateau: Nez Percé, Walla Walla, Yakama, Umatilla, Flathead, Spokan, Okanagon

California Intermountain: Paiute, Ute, Shoshone, Klamath, Yurok, Patwin, Wintun

Great Plains: Blackfoot, Mandan, Sioux, Cheyenne, Arapaho, Shoshone, Comanche

Eastern Woodlands: Iroquois, Delaware; Micmac, Narragansett, Shawnee, Potawatomi

Southeast: Cherokee, Choctaw, Chickasaw, Creek, Seminole

Southwest: Navajo, Apache, Havasupai, Mojave

Mesoamerica: Olmec, Maya, Aztec

The Tale of the Pig

BACKGROUND

Most of the folk tales that became popular as fairy tales and crossed the Atlantic to America did so largely because of the publication of the writings of Jacob and Wilhelm Grimm in the early 1800s. It was their idea to compile the folk tales that they grew up with in Germany and give them simple morals. This inspired other writers, including Scotland's Andrew Lang and Denmark's Hans Christian Andersen, all across Europe to do the same. With the stories in print, and being translated into all the European languages, these now common tales could reach across borders and be compared to stories of one's own land. In "The Tale of the Pig," it is easy to find themes that are present in many other European tales, many that we have grown up with and know by heart.

The concept of magic or magical beings is prevalent in many folk tales and myths, including some in this book, such as "Feet Water" and "The Golden Reed Pipe." This is, however, the only folk tale play in this book that involves an animal whose magical powers are considered unusual. According to folk tradition, a character's unusual powers are not meant to be believed or taken literally. Instead, they serve to accentuate a lesson or moral. In this tale, the contrast between the lowly appearance of the pig-prince and his wonderful, creative personality helps drive home this story's simple morals of trusting others, not judging a book by its cover, and being content with what you have.

> ### VOCABULARY
>
> Romania   emperor
> palace   disguise

STAGING TIPS

In staging this play, consider the fun ways that the bridge could be built from the snout of the pig. Some carefully positioned balls of yarn thrown from behind the pig could serve this purpose very well. Be sure to take the imaginations of the audience into consideration when producing the pig's costume. A simple snout with elastic conveys the idea wonderfully and allows the actor to take it off and put it back on easily.

The Tale of the Pig

◆ CHARACTERS ◆

The Storyteller	Emperor's Guard
Old Man	Emperor
Old Woman	Empress
The Pig	Princess

The Storyteller: A *fairy tale* is a kind of folk tale that is very popular in the United States. Most people in America grow up hearing stories like "Cinderella" or "Little Red Ridinghood." But most of these stories have been brought to America from other countries. This next story is a fairy tale from Romania that is similar to a story you may have heard, "The Frog Prince." This time, however, the prince is not a frog, but a pig.

Once upon a time there lived a very old couple. The husband was 100 years old and his wife was 90.

(*Old Man and Old Woman are finishing dinner.*)

Old Man: Mother, dinner tonight was delicious!

Old Woman: Thank you, Father. I liked it too.

Old Man: Mother, I have a question for you. Why do I call you Mother and you call me Father, when we have no children between us?

Old Woman: You're right, Father. We should have a child. Tomorrow when you are on your way home from town, pick up the first creature you find and bring it home. Then we will have a child of our very own!

The Storyteller: The old man went into town the next day, and on his way home he spotted a family of pigs. One pig was smaller than the others. He was scrawny and skinny and could not keep up with the other pigs. The old man picked up this little pig and brought it home to his wife.

(Old Woman cradles the pig in her arms.)

Old Woman: What a beautiful child we have! He looks just like you, Father.

The Storyteller: The old woman was happy to have the pig for her son. She washed and fed it and nursed it back to health. When other people saw the pig and laughed she would say,

Old Woman: This is my son! He is different from everyone else!

The Storyteller: One day some important news traveled throughout the kingdom. The emperor was looking for a husband for his daughter, the princess.

Old Woman: How wonderful! The princess should get married and have beautiful children of her own. Of course, even a princess could not have a child as beautiful as our son.

Old Man: Mother, you haven't heard the whole story! The emperor has decided that only the man who is able to build a bridge from his own house to the palace may marry the princess. This bridge must be made of gold and paved with jewels and lined with trees and singing birds from all over the world.

Old Woman: How lovely!

Old Man: Except that any man who tries to build the bridge and fails will have his head where his ankles are faster than you can say, "Our son is a piglet, not a prince!"

Old Woman: Our son is a prince if we say he is a prince!

Old Man: It is a good thing our son can't speak. He won't be tempted to try any foolish bridge building.

The Pig: Snort! Father, I can build it.

Old Man: Who said that?

The Pig: I did.

(*Old Woman faints.*)

Old Man: Pig? How is it that you speak? Look, you've made your mother faint.

The Pig: My mother will be happy when I build that bridge and she sees who I really am. Snort. Please take me to the emperor's palace. I have a princess to marry!

The Storyteller: The old man agreed and traveled to the palace with the pig skipping happily behind him. But a guard stopped them when they reached the palace gate.

Emperor's Guard: Old man, what do you want?

(*Old Man bows.*)

Old Man: I have brought my son to see the emperor. He can build the bridge that the emperor wants.

The Pig: Snort!

Emperor's Guard: Your son? You are a foolish old man. That is nothing but a pig!

Old Man: Just the same, he is my son. Please let me see the emperor.

The Storyteller: The guard let the old man into the palace.

(*Old Man bows to the emperor.*)

Emperor: I hear that your son can build my bridge.

Old Man: Yes, sir, he says that he can.

Emperor: When may I meet your son?

Old Man: He is right here, sir.

The Pig: Snort!

Emperor: That is nothing but a pig!

Old Man: It is my son, sir, and he says that he can build your bridge.

Emperor: I must say that I am curious. Old man, tell your son that he has until tomorrow to build my bridge. If he fails, it is you, old man, who will have your head at your ankles by sundown.

The Storyteller: Worried, the old man went home with his son.

The Pig: Don't worry, Father. I can build that bridge. Snort. Then you will see who I really am.

The Storyteller: When they got home, the old man told his wife what had happened. Before she could say a word, the pig went to the window and stuck his head outside. He took a great big breath in and then blew out hard through his snout. Right before their eyes, out of the breath of the pig, the emperor's bridge was formed of solid gold. When the old man and woman looked at each other, they were no longer dressed in rags, but in royal robes. The old cottage turned into a palace even bigger than the emperor's palace. The pig ran across the bridge to get his bride.

The Pig: Snort! I've come for the princess!

Emperor: I don't know how you did it, but this is the bridge I ordered. Daughter, this is your new husband.

Princess: But, Papa, he's a pig! Gross!

Emperor: I know, but he was able to do an impossible task. And an emperor is only as good as his word. Besides, it's obvious he has magic powers. You must go and live with him right away or he might turn his power against us.

The Storyteller: The princess went to live with the pig and his parents. That night when the pig climbed into bed he took off his pigskin and the princess saw that he was really a handsome prince. As time went on, the princess got used to the pig being a pig by day and a prince at night, but she was still embarrassed to be seen with him in his pigskin. One day she went back to her parents' palace and told them about the pig-prince.

Emperor: I know that you are not happy with a pig for a husband, but you must not do anything to anger him. He has fantastic magic that he uses!

Empress: Nonsense! My dear daughter, you should not be seen with that silly pig! It is our luck that he is a prince in disguise. What you must do is keep a fire on the stove at all times. When the prince is asleep, sneak out of your bed and throw that nasty pigskin into the fire.

Emperor: No, no! That will anger the pig for sure!

Empress: He is a prince, not a pig!

Emperor: But he has powers! There is nothing scarier than a powerful pig!

The Storyteller: The princess went home and thought about her parents' advice. She could not understand why anyone would want to live like a pig, so she took her mother's advice. One night, while the prince was sleeping, she sneaked out of bed, stole the pigskin, and threw it into the fire. When the prince awoke, he was very angry.

The Pig: What have you done? You have listened to the advice of others and brought great misfortune to my parents and to us! You deserve neither prince nor pig!

The Storyteller: Suddenly, there was a strong wind and the bridge cracked and crumbled. The old couple's robes turned back to rags and their house became an old cottage once again. The prince was gone in a gust of wind.

Old Woman: I was content to have a son, no matter what he was or was not. Now, Princess, because you could not be happy with what you had, I have lost my son.

Old Man: I have lost my castle.

Princess: I have lost my husband.

The Storyteller: The old couple sent the princess back to her family, as they had no way to support her anymore, and she never did marry again. The old couple chose to remain content with their life just as it was. But still, they thought of a life of riches every time they passed a farm and heard the pigs squeal. Snort!

The Tale of the Pig

SOCIAL STUDIES ◆ *Many Leaders*

Ask students what they know about the differences among an emperor, a sultan, a king, a president, and other types of leaders. Discuss how different cultures have different leaders: *Do they all do the same job? How are governments structured differently from one another?* Students might choose one type of leader and find out which countries have that kind of leader. For younger students, you might begin by accessing what students know best: the rules at home. Ask: *What is the "government" structure of your family? Who makes the rules? How is the government of a family different than the government of a country?*

LANGUAGE ARTS
◆ *What Happens Next?*

Ask students to write a paragraph or two from the point of view of one of the characters of this play. The paragraphs should begin where the play leaves off. For example, what happens to the old couple now that they are childless again? Where does the pig-prince go? What happens to the princess when she gets back to her parents' palace? A wonderful example of this type of writing is *The Frog Prince, Continued* by Jon Scieszka.

THEATER ◆ *Walk Like/Talk Like*

There are a wide variety of characters in this play—old ones (the old couple), young ones (the princess), powerful ones (the emperor), and even animals (the pig). Learning about how you can change your body to create a character is an important part of acting. Ask students to walk across the room as if they were an old person, a pig, and so forth. How does each character move differently from the others? Then try speaking. Give the students a simple line of dialogue to say and have them repeat it as each character.

SCIENCE ◆ *Skin Shedding*

In "The Tale of the Pig" the pig "sheds" his skin to reveal that he is really a prince. Do pigs really shed their skin? What are some animals that do? In what way do furry animals shed? What about people? Use this chapter to create a lesson on skin and its properties (see Resources).

◆ RESOURCES ◆

Cuts, Breaks, Bruises, and Burns: How Your Body Heals by Joanna Cole (Crowell, 1985).

I Wonder Why Snakes Shed Their Skins and Other Questions About Reptiles by Amanda O'Neill (Kingfisher Books, 1996).

The Frog Prince, Continued by Jon Scieszka (Puffin, 1994).

BillNye.com at www.nylabs.kcts.org Search NyeLabs Episode Guide index for SKIN.

Glossary of Theater Terms

Acting area: The area within the performance space where the actor moves in full view of the audience.

Apron: Section of the stage floor which projects toward or into the auditorium.

Backstage: The part of the stage and theater that is out of the sight of the audience.

Blackout: Shut down of stage lighting.

Blocking: The arrangement of moves to be made by the actors during the play.

Costume: The clothes actors wear to make them look like the characters they are playing.

Cue: The signal an actor uses to say a line or make a movement.

Director: The person in charge of running rehearsals and making decisions about the actors and the play. (The boss.)

Downstage: The part of the stage nearest to the audience.

Dress rehearsal: Usually the last rehearsal. Will be just like the play in performance.

House: Another word for the audience or the auditorium.

Offstage: A motion near the closest side of the stage from the middle.

Props (properties): Furnishings, set dressings, and any other item which will be used in the course of the play. Props that are mostly kept on an actor's person are known as personal props.

Script: The book that contains the lines and movements of the play.

Set: The furnishings and backdrop needed to create the environment in which the play takes place.

Spotlight: A light that shines on a group of people or one person on stage.

Stage left/right: Left and right sides of the stage from an actor's point of view when looking at the audience.

Stage manager: The person in charge of making sure things get done in rehearsal and during the play.

Upstage: The part of the stage farthest from the audience.